Life

on

Earth:

The Game

**a Manual for those
who didn't bring theirs**

RANDALL C. SHELTON

OnlyUno Publishers
Redmond, Oregon

ONLY UNO PUBLISHERS
© 2007 by Randall C. Shelton

Published by: Only Uno Publishers
P.O. Box 2430
Redmond, OR 97756

Printed in the United States of America by
Maverick Publications • Bend, Oregon

Cover art and illustrations by
Tim Donahue

ISBN: 978-0-9795886-0-0

" TIME OUT ! "

SOURCE View:

Playing Field A.
Game One,
No Penalties ...

" Your Move "

This manual is dedicated to
every human on Earth who ever asked either openly
or just quietly to themselves,

"Who am I? What is my purpose?"

This manual is provided for
all those students who are unknowingly ready.

Since you have read this far, you are included.

This Manual is an abridged version of the orientation,
guidance, and planning in which you participated prior to
your entry into this kosmic Game—Life on Earth.
Due to the expansive parameters and rules of The Game,
however, specific guidance is omitted.

Contents

Illustrations by Tim Donahue

Message to the Reader

Peruse this material as you would pore over a map seeking new places to discover, even though these places are only waiting to be RE-discovered. You will find that there is a beautiful place within your being, which when "seeing" that place will cause your heart to sing and soul cry with joy. Your journey will then be recognized for what it is and has been, and will take on a new color and meaning.

Welcome to your new map.

Welcome to your rediscovery of
Who You Really Are.

Read in anticipation and expectancy, resulting in a quiet change unto the beautiful new YOU.

Preface

Most everyone at one time or another ponders the meaning of life. You probably have; I certainly have. Thousands of books delve into various aspects of life's meaning; some even imply that they hold the answer. Most are, when we evaluate them, from the opinions of thinkers from the past. I use the word "opinions," for that is mostly what anything in print is: an opinion of the author. These, normally based on what those writers have read (and rearranged); which was many times, the opinions of other thinkers and researchers.

Admittedly, this manual is my opinion. However, this is primarily the result of my experience, and therein lies a major difference. Voluminous reading along the way opened me up to accepting other arenas, bringing on more experiences, and verifying pieces—other aspects of the puzzle, that puzzle, of course, being "What is this life all about?"

This manual is the culmination of over thirty years of deliberate questioning and seeking. Years which often took me into rooms of information seldom explored by mainstream academia. During that time, I found that hundreds of people have had life experiences similar to my own. After sifting the evidence which shows up from different angles of orientation, it must be investigated. The areas of my research spanned across the religious and through the paranormal. That research was not by reading books, but through actual experiences. A quick excursion into a side arena of UFOs, provided pieces to the ever-enlarging puzzle as did exposure into crop circles. The jury is still out on both subjects as they almost immediately linked to a head-on confrontation with quantum mechanics and all its mysteries. These all continued to expand as did my personal experiences. Yes, even as this is being written, I'm ever onward up the spiral.

No specific "cul de sacs of interest" of a particular topic held me for long periods of time. No specific author's views held a position of "the answer." Instead, they all opened avenues to possible answers. Discovery of the big picture has been the impetus and basis for my search, and I must tell you, it has been an amazing journey.

The statement "Here is the answer" implies an absolute. Such is not possible in this ever-changing, ever-growing, ever-challenging set of options presented to us in this life on Earth. As I see it, regardless of what others insist on telling us, there is no "answer" per se. I offer you here the story of how I've come to these, my momentary conclusions. And where possible how I have arrived at what is in this manual—"the one" you didn't bring with you.

This, our life on Earth is complex, to say the least. Every thinking player is aware of that fact, and most players are struggling with those complexities—struggling rather than using them to their advantage. That would be similar to swimming against the current of a fast moving river rather than using it to your advantage.

You might be wondering to yourself, "Gee, Randall, that sounds pretty serious. On what are you basing all this?"

And my answer is… it's all in this manual. Simply read through, page by page, taking note of the recommendations as you read. And please, place your ever-present judgments up on a shelf. Just set them aside for the time being.

"Well, why would you ask that? Everybody has his or her own opinions and beliefs about everything," you might insist.

That's just it. That's why I ask you to be open minded right up to the ending. Skipping ahead is not recommended, so just read page by page and savor these mental morsels.

This manual is like nothing you've ever read. And, as you will discover, it's more a reference manual than a how-to manual. On a very special level this is an exposé on the nature of and reasons for both planet Earth and the humans who inhabit it.

What Brought This Whole Thing On?

Three incidents in my life helped to ignite an unsuspecting and ever-growing curiosity. They ultimately lead to the publication of this manual. But my journey started long before that.

For many of us, our early years were spent being exposed to (or immersed in) one religious dogma or another. Such was my case. I was almost raised *in* the Methodist Church, with the Holy Bible (King James version, of course) and the Methodist Hymnal. As a child I went to Sunday School, as I got older it was Youth Fellowship, and I even sang in the choir. This enabled me to hear a lot of sermons by a variety of preachers. My college major was Religious Education, it included both Baker University in eastern Kansas and the University of Denver, where I graduated class of 1955. One particular class at Baker was "Life and Teachings of Jesus" taught by a rather radical professor. (He "kept on" about the virgin birth.) Years later, I realized just how subtle his interests were regarding various segments of Jesus' life and how they could have ignited far more interest for me had I, the student, been ready. Unbeknownst to me, those classes subtly pointed me toward my blueprint. (You have a blueprint for your life too.)

However, in the mid 1970s, as I see it now, my blueprint moved to the foreground (ahhh, the benefits of hindsight!).

After a conversation with one of her "flying partners," my new partner and wife, Linda, suggested we have psychic readings. "Sure, I'm easy," was probably my reply. Another highly recommended psychic provided a second reading. It too was good but one particular reference to a "past life" setting off "waves of warm", is all I can say. This soon pushed me with more than mild curiosity to a book about Edgar Cayce. Brad Steiger's book *Atlantis Rising* was next. I recalled reading (earlier), all about Bridey Murphy and how she was smeared (literally) all over the news; therefore, reading books of a different "ilk" as I call it, became an even stronger draw for me. After reading another book by Brad Steiger, I was then referred to *Seth* by Jane Roberts. This one I carefully studied and found fascinating along with a delightful little gem *Space , Time and Beyond* by Toben & Wolf. I picked up *Messages from Michael* by Chelsea Yarbro which was "coincidentally"a precursor to a significant segment of my future learning. The flow then increased rapidly, due to having taken instruction in and working with the Evelyn Woods Reading Dynamics program in the late 1960s. More books. Authors such as Marilyn Ferguson, Carlos Castaneda, Shakti Gawain, Ruth Montgomery, Dr. Paul Brunton, and Gary Zukav (and his *Dancing Wu Li Masters*). The reading train built up momentum. The more I read, the more I wanted to know. The ensuing torrent of input included Ramtha, Yogananda, Louise Hay, David Hawkins, Deepak Chopra, Vitvan, Dr. Joel Whitton, Joseph Campbell, a newsletter named "Homewords" from Trance-Channeler, Susan Johansen (aka Sheradon Bryce and her "Joyriding the Universe") and others. The blueprint had given notice, but only subconsciously. During this time, Linda and I purchased our first home and I had invited myself into an ESP group.

When Neale Donald Walsch showed up on the scene, things seemed to go into high gear. Michael Talbot's book *The Holographic Universe* had a part to play, also. Esther and Jerry Hicks and Abraham: that wonderful trio also disclosed additional pieces for my puzzle. All those books laid the foundation for the key pieces that changed the direction of my life. But now I'm getting ahead of myself.

First, I had readings by those two separate psychics, and whose readings stacked up some kindling for an eventual firestorm in my personal life of searching. Searching for what? At the time, if you would have asked me I couldn't have answered you. I just became interested in knowing more.

The second incident that had a profound effect on me was a never-to-be-forgotten evening of working on the Ouija board. After researching and evaluating it from strictly personal experience under trusting conditions, I found the practice of using a Ouija board to be a credible, worthwhile, and useful tool to communicate with (literally) unsuspected dimensions—amazing discoveries. The secret to successfully working with a Ouija board depends totally on (a) one's intent and (b) the belief stance of associates in the room.

The third incident occurred while in a meditation group. I had the amazing experience of feeling, in each hand, volley ball-sized orbiting energies. Yes, I know it sounds a bit "far-fetched", as my Grandma Tucker would say, but it's true. This, of course, added additional fuel to the now unquenchable fire of desiring to become better informed. Again, about *what*—I could not have told you.

As I look back at my life, my interests were tickled in the late 1950s when a palm reading given to two couples of us, displayed uncanny accuracy. The friendly lady had learned the skill in India while accompanying her spouse on a temporary corporate transfer. We knew nothing of them and they knew nothing of us nor have I seen her since that evening at a very nice restaurant on East Colfax in Denver. (That was back when there was such a thing.) The woman accurately deciphered information from the palms of each one of us. In fact, her readings "nailed" all four of us. Her husband sat patiently waiting for her to finish. I suspect he had been through the drill before.

My first Ouija board experience was a real eye opener. I sat and watched two "sensitives" (psychics when they allowed it) whom I met months prior, as they softly placed their fingers

on the planchette. Immediately; almost frantic, the instrument bolted back and forth across the board. The ladies were
even amazed at the force being displayed. Finally after recording by pencil a legal tablet page of letters which looked like
non words, I asked for a break—to review. As we scanned the
page of a, m, k, c, e and o's minus punctuation, of course, I
noted two definite words. Interestingly enough they were re-
peated: "run, run, beer, beer."

We decided to allow this as "someone's" attempt to communicate. We verbally acknowledged our acceptance and
recognition. We then commenced upon a very unsuspecting
"conversation". Over the course of the next several minutes
we determined that the spirit attempting to communicate
(from his name) was a male. He had been killed in Colorado
by a car, but not one that he was in. He disclosed he was 18 at
the time of death.

The experience of being torn away from one's body unexpect-
edly must have been terribly shocking, so much so that he did
not realize that he was supposed to pass to the other side.
Instead he remained disoriented and apparently somewhat lost
in between worlds and apparently passing through the folds of
time.

In a learning experience for us all, we were able to assist in his
moving to the Light, so he was no longer frightened or frus-
trated at the conclusion of our contact. I deduced this, based
on further 'conversation' prior to his moving the planchette
to 'bye'. (This was over 25 years before "the Ghost Whisperer,"
remember.)

That evening turned into a beautiful experience for the seven
of us 'on this side' and hopefully for him. But even moreso, no
doubt for the other Light 'consciousness' which had apparently been with him throughout his wandering. It was
undoubtedly just waiting for him to acknowledge it. I only
wish I had asked more questions. If you want the complete
story let me know on our blog: onlyuno.blogspot.com

The following Monday I called the Colorado State Patrol, talked with a lady in their records section and gave her the brief particulars about the incident. I said nothing about the beer. Two days later she called me back and read to me all the details of the incident—directly from the report. It was just as he described them to us. She read "they had been drinking beer"—and naturally the bells went off. The date of the fateful occurrence interestingly enough was five years previous to my call. Although I went into that evenings experience a somewhat skeptic, curiosity allowed the door to be open. That evenings experience resulted in many more exciting, albeit non-ordinary, experiences.

Following that mind-opening evening, the experiences had both individually and collectively by the members of the Circle of Light were beyond belief. Many other communications with spirit were allowed as possibilities, with more than a few "placed on the shelf," since we had no way of proving them. We did tape all our sessions. It was not at all uncommon to find us looking through maps and encyclopedias.

Contact of an entirely different kind occurred over many months via automatic writing done by a trusted friend and psychic while in trance. Watching and questioning during those experiences, week after week, then month after month resulted in an accumulation of information, which became a pivotal point in my concluding that there was definitely something to this.

Some was verifiable, while with other material: no confirming sources were available—here on Earth, anyhow. The members of the Friday night Circle of Light (we met for fifteen years) became quite accustomed to Kay's* automatic writing style while in trance. She initially used her left hand, even though she was not left handed and *Kay is not her real name.

One particular Friday evening, we experienced something truly awesome. All ten of us were touched to our very core. The full and complete story of this will be detailed in an E-book in the very near future. But here's the story in a nutshell. Kay was seated and in her 'normal' deep trance state. Upon seeing the following words (while standing in my normal position behind and reading over her shoulder) written slowly and carefully upon the legal pad in her lap; "Thou art with me at last," the scope of my entire life changed. Why? During one of those psychic readings that I had sat through two years previously, a reference was made alluding to a life as a Roman soldier. I was no longer just overly curious. I felt an indescribable rekindling of a relationship from another life experience the moment I read those words out loud. Leaving for home late that evening there was no doubt, I was now on a re-directed journey. This manual is a major segment of that path.

Twenty-seven years later my interest is even stronger. The following offering, an excerpt from *"And the Word Became Flesh,"* found on page 21-22 which came to me four years after that awesome evening will help to explain why it has now become not only my life's journey but also the cause for this manual and its title.

> *This is your priority one. This is why you came here this time. You now know. Actually you have known for some time and have been avoiding the truth of it, due to the ongoing glitter and glamour inherent in The Game.*

As you continue to read through this manual, clarification of points in that passage will be provided, as will my full story, and in it you just may find some of it to be your story also.

In philosophical circles there is a well-known saying: "When the student is ready the teacher will appear." After those experiences, I was ready.   Are you?

The following three disclosures encapsulate the essence of this manual. This could even be our starting point because this manual just gets better from here.

Disclosure #1
You don't remember this, but YOU are a participant in a gigantic game. By "gigantic" I mean a game of cosmic proportions. Cosmic—as in our Milky Way galaxy being a mere segment of the referenced scope. It's in "Universe 45" according to some 'sources'.

Disclosure #2
You voluntarily *chose* to become a player in this game and if any judgment takes place—you will do it. The practice is discouraged, however.

Disclosure #3
The basic reason you don't remember: The Game is designed to stall your recall.
Obviously, it is designed to take all comers. Every person on the planet is playing this Game, and yes, most are totally unaware of any of this information.

Did you suspect you were in a game?

Especially, one of cosmic proportions?

Clarifications

S ome of the words I use are not used in the normal way or do not have the normal spelling, so let me explain.

I would prefer to hyphenate "human" because You are occupying a "physical form powered by a unique light energy." Light takes on different hues, so hu-man is akin to hue-man. You designed your body (in which you are presently living) and planned your life in general with assistance prior to entry into The Game. Each unit of consciousness sets out and designs what it intends to achieve.[1]

I use the word "blueprint" in an unusual context here. We all know that buildings under construction are completed as a result of planning, design, and hard work. So it is with the anticipated life of every spiritual being as it chooses to take on human form. Before you enter into The Game, you plan out what, in general you want to accomplish. You draw up a plan for your life. But keep in mind that you have free will and may even forget your blueprint, temporarily.

We came to the awareness of blueprints after reviewing among other sources, case histories of people who have voluntarily undergone regression hypnosis. Those cases routinely indicate

---

[1] Michael Newton's "Journey of Souls" plus his other books.

that one's plan for life on Earth is self designed, not imposed. The totality of one's life results from, in all probability, a combination of many elements including (a) our preplanning prior to entry along with (b) perceptions we arrive at from the coaching we were and are exposed to, (especially as a 'mere babe'), as well as prevalent, invasive thoughts; many coming to us as emotions from the sea of mass consciousness. Our internal and ever-present power of attraction then places circumstances upon our plate of options–all to be dealt with, strictly as we choose. It is no wonder that we sometimes feel as though we are being ganged up on.

The phrase "glitter and glamour" describes the ever-existing and continually increasing distractions ever prevalent within The Game. Distracting all individuals and causing them to think they don't have time for many things, *quiet time in particular*. Glitter and Glamour increase the probability that The Game could be winning by helping you to remain in your ongoing state of amnesia.

"Kosmos"spelled thusly, is now a favorite word of mine. Ken Wilber uses it liberally. Ken's spelling and references to the word come from the Greek, meaning everything from cellular to intergalactic.[2]

"Offering" refers to a gift, which is available to whoever chooses to accept it. An offering: as with hands out, palms up, arms outstretched. Offering is used when referring to a book, a short writing, or an illustration.

An amazing skill which I was introduced to, called thought-plane transference is akin to channeling. It is, I'm sure, experienced by many poets, musicians and writers. Mozart excelled at it. Once one becomes quiet, allowing, and focused, an amazing connection with every interested beautiful unit of consciousness in the universe may BE. The challenge is to become truly quiet, because mental discipline is required. One

---

[2] See bibliography "Integral Spirituality"

must create a place for the chatter in the cranium to be slowly and surely set aside. Then, just listen. It's simple. Simple, but not necessarily easy. The key is trusting in it. Specific offerings in italics throughout this manual were received by the author and are offered to you. More may be found on our website: www.onlyuno.com.

To enable you to bring on a non-image when referencing THE (unable-to-be-labeled-or-described) CREATOR OF ALL THAT IS, I have selected the word "Source." The word Source is used in place of All, Allah, God, It, Tao or whatever you choose to call your Creator. After you finish reading this manual you will realize why. Also we'll clarify why "we" is used in appropriate places rather than "I".

Rest assured: we do not intend that this material refute anyone's religious beliefs. Perhaps (and hopefully) it will expand those beliefs as a result of your viewing them from a different perspective.

You will notice nonstandard capitalization throughout, especially in my personal offerings. Terms such as "Source," "The Game," and "The Partner" are capitalized because they refer to the spiritual, nondual, unlimited meanings of those terms, not the everyday, earthbound meanings. Furthermore, "you" refers to your lower, ego self, whereas YOU refers to your higher, divine self—the one that knows who you really are. This may be confusing on first reading but study and thought should clarify the issue.

The life of which we truly "are" is—as is Source—unable to label. However we must label it—something.

I've chosen "energy" but it's not the energy most all engineers reference. "Fields" are a necessary part of their energy designations. The energy of which we "are" is not field related. So—just know WE ARE Undefinable, Indescribable Kosmic Energy. UIKE ? Hmmm.

Why do I call life on Earth a Game? Life is serious business, after all, not something frivolous, right? The following quote from Nobel laureate Rabindranath Tagore suggests why this whole experience is probably a game.

> "A game is a game where there is a player to play it. Of course, there is a law of the game, which it is of use to us to analyze and to master. But, if it be asserted that in this law is its reality, then we cannot accept it. For the game is what it is to the players. The game changes its aspects according to the personality of its players; for some its end is the lust of gain, in others that of applause; some finding it the means for satisfying their social instinct, and there are others who approach it in the spirit of dis-interested curiosity for studying its secrets. Yet all through its manifold aspects its law remains the same. For the nature of reality is the variedness of its unity. And the world is like this game to us—it is the same and yet it is not the same to us all."

> —Rabindranath Tagore 1861-1941

Many agree: Tagore is a poet of great wisdom, although he probably wouldn't qualify as light reading. The book I have was given to me by a young lady at our second ever, casual meeting. At the time I wondered why and then not too long after that, I heard she had "passed on". An interesting... "coincidence."

One extremely interesting publication if you can find it—is titled The Emerald Tablets. The following is from the Tablets and is a worthwhile place from which to embark:

> "On Earth, man is in bondage. Bound by space and time to the earth plane. Encircling each planet a wave of vi-bration binds him to his plane of unfoldment. Yet, within man is the key to releasement. Within man may freedom be found. Bound are ye in your body, but by thy power ye may be free. This is the secret whereby bondage shall be replaced by freedom for thee."

I find carefully placed within this quotation a key to the formula of winning this Game. That formula may truly release man (the physical form powered by kosmic light energy) to find his innate freedom and enable him to win The Game. It also hints at another truth regarding all kosmic life: quite simply, potentially all players in this Game are in control of their own future.

....Just how that is realized, you may find in the pages of this manual.

Most manuals are not very wordy. As you will find, this one is a bit different. Most manuals don't have unusual artwork. This one, as you will see, does. And YOU are the reason, as you will see.

As you are exposed to both the concepts and the art, you will realize this is not an everyday, run-of-the-mill manual. That's why we stated on the back cover, "After reading this, you will never see life the same way again." And, I should add, you may never see *yourself* the same way again.

What Others Have to Say

Shhhh... it will come to you

Tim Donahue, during his creative tenure in Hollywood was nominated (4) four times for Emmy awards and he enjoys being a two time winner. The synchronicity that brought us together is a story in itself. His professionalism and imagination show in everything he creates, as is displayed in the amazing illustrations and the covers of our manual. All throughout this publication process his assistance has been invaluable. We thank him for wanting to be a part of this work and anticipate joining in other creative endeavors with him, very soon.

Tim requested that he be included in this section. This is his offering as he wrote it.

> When I was a kid, my 7-year-older brother used to take me to the movies. They scared the yell out of me often at night. It's a game we played with ourselves. My brother was a great game player. I wasn't.

> In grade school, my teacher gave us a test one day from things that she had said earlier. But, when someone in the class asked her, "How am I supposed to remember everything that you ever say?" her reply was a puzzle to me. Later in life it paid off big time (as Life often does for us). She said, "Shhhhhh! It will come to you."

When the other student argued, she would say, "Shhhhh... quiet. It will come to you."

Well, I had seen a movie called "IT—the Terror from Beyond Space," and maybe it was only a guy in a spikey-tooth-filled rubber-scaled movie costume with big buggy eyes and claws, but all I could think of was how I didn't want "IT" to come to ME!!! In fact, nothing came to me that day. Needless to say, I didn't pass the test that day, and I haven't passed a lot of tests in my life for similar reasons. Reason: I'm always thinking about something else—something I'd rather be doing. I've probably been one of many in the world who doesn't know HOW the "Game" is played. Fortunately, there ARE those who do know and we'll sometimes find them when we aren't even trying. Not to worry, they're going to find you. It's in the Rules somewhere...but I never read that book.

Now, all of a sudden I'm working on a book! Me??

"Why me?" I asked Randall.

"When you're working on your artwork, it will begin to come to you. Just allow it to come in. Open up the windows. Just open up," he said. "Allow. Find you some quiet time. And it will come to you."

The Universe is talking to me now. I can hear it! Some AMAZING things have happened to me recently. I don't even try to imagine how. So, I want you to meet my friend Randall, One of the most amazing Space Creatures that I've ever met in my life. So wonderful, so loving, so nurturing, and so peaceful and non-moody. (Where the heck did he come from?) I found him ...well, we found our wives and they introduced us. I found what I've been looking for all my life. "What is it?" you ask. Ha! Just You WAIT! Have FUN. En-JOY.

—Tim Donahue, Artist, Seeker, Believer

Tim also wrote the introductory comments to each of his illustrations. He is one very talented human being.

From a Long Time Friend and Fellow Seeker

Mrs. Sandra Lund, the author of *The Kyrian Letters* is married to a talented and successful artist, Denton Lund, and they live in Wyoming. When I told her about this publication, Sandy asked to be included. Her comments which follow are self-explanatory, and we cannot thank her enough for them.

"On page 30 of this refreshing life manual, Randall makes reference to a group called Universalia. This group came together in 1981 while we were all living in Colorado. Randall and his wife, Linda, were among the original members of that weekly metaphysical study group. I have known the author for 27 years and during the seven years that the group met regularly, I became familiar with his character, his personality, his inquiring mind, his spiritual seeking, his unique sense of humor, and his original writing style.

Universalia was a group of truth-seeking strangers who came together and, in essence, formed a family. Not only did the members of this study group meet weekly for those seven years, we also published a newsletter, *The Universalian*, We also created annual symposia and were instrumental in the formation of other Universalia groups across the Front Range of Colorado. When people work together, play together, create together and even disagree at times, you come to know the heart of another. Randall was a completely involved participant and we all knew him at his heart level.

Randall and Linda were more than members of the group; they became treasured friends on my life journey. I can speak of Randall as one who knows him at his heart level. He is family, he is friend; he is a fellow traveler in life. As a person, he is intelligent, cheerful, curious, open minded, and fun loving. As a friend, he is loyal and caring. As a writer, his style is uniquely his own. I listened to and read his offerings for many years. Those writings were always deep and thought provoking. One of the finest and, perhaps, the most credible quality he has as a writer is that of integrity. He is totally honest in what he shares. He studies, he researches, he explores, and he is absolutely connected to and trusts that highest part of himself. And from that inner sanctuary, from out of the quietness of his being, he shares, I am sure, what has been given from the Source of All Life."

Sandy was the key member in our Universalia group. Among her many talents, she compiled and edited our newsletter, which went out worldwide—and this was before the internet. When you go to Denton and Sandy's website at www.dentonlund.com you will find it a very beautiful place to visit. Sandy expertly designed and created that website for Denton's artistic creations. Here is an excerpt from Sandy's book, *The Kyrian Letters*, which is full of amazing subjects to mull over in your quiet time.

> "When you come to the true awareness that the real you is energy and spirit and not form, you will be released from fear. You will be released from fear when you acknowledge Who You Really Are: a Spirit of God. His own Essence. The physical walk is but a short journey in terms of time, and there is so much beauty ahead. Fear is released when you replace it with Love, the healing and transforming energy of the Cosmos. This is your whole purpose on the Full Circle Journey: to love; to learn it, to teach it and to be it."

Why This Manual Right Now?

The following offering is placed here for two reasons—first, as another explanation for what has taken place on the planet regarding Love Energy, and second, to indicate what may be "coming up the road" at us.

And the Word Became Flesh

The energy became flesh in order to function upon the planet earth. The word, "word" was inserted due to the fact that energy was unknown per se when the scribes were collecting all those stories. To them, the energy of HIS love was of such a concentrated degree it was obvious to all who witnessed it that there was definitely something amazingly different in the personage of the One exuding it. Thus the legends.[3]

That love energy is once again becoming evident upon the planet. It is within the lives of many sleepers who are gaining their wakefulness. How this is taking place is of no consequence at this point. The mere fact that the situation is "turning around" is what is of consequence. Reassurance is of significance to those who are awakening. This is due to the fact that their awakening is on an individual basis. They have no one to reassure them. They have no one they may confirm their inclinations with.

An emerging of the book is now of import. Founded upon the love factor—tied to the partnership and explained within the "manual" will be the peace that is needed for them to walk with assurance and trust their inner knowing. The acquisition of this information for them will not be your concern. Merely get clarification into a readable, constructive and completed form. This is the task now. The completion of the book is paramount. Now.

Many are wondering as to the "why" of their existence. The manual explains that. Others are in a place of wanting clarification on the true meaning of love and its implications upon the planet. Others are straying from the clear truth of the relationship of their partnering with the Light Source of ALL.

The horrible indignities done to the minds of far too many peoples upon the planet regarding their true essence must be clarified. Now. The slipshod manner in which the self-appointed spiritual leaders

---

[3] Refers I believe, to Buddha, Jesus, Mohammed, etc.

are instructing their flocks is reaching to the point of too little too late…thus it is important that the epistle be made available to the masses, a.s.a.p., as you say.

This is your priority one. This is why you came here this time. You now know. Actually you have known for some time and have been avoiding the truth of it… due to the ongoing glitter and glamour inherent in The Game.

Question: If you received such a notice as this, what would you do?

"Well.......it would depend upon just who it was that laid this ultimatum on me. . . . . Right ?"

Right. I have a good idea as to just 'who' it was that placed that notice in front of me. We have been communicating for quite some time. So now you understand another facet of the reason for this manual. The information in this publication is a compilation of decades of study and practice—of all kinds.

And From Other Sources

In addition to receiving inner guidance, I received "outer" guidance in the form of other well-known authors "pulling back the curtains" and inadvertently disclosing a beautifully different slant on the subject of why this manual is now made available. The following excerpt is from chapter three in the book entitled *Tomorrow's God*, by Neale Donald Walsch, who is the author of the *Conversations With God* series. Here, we're eavesdropping on a conversation between God and Neale. God, "in quotations" is speaking. Neale's questioning is indicated [in brackets.]

"Humanity's future depends on what humanity thinks about God, and about Life.
From your thought springs your reality. From your ideas your future emerges. Thus, your beliefs create your behaviors, and your behaviors create your experience.

What you believe, therefore, becomes the most important thing."

[What creates beliefs? Can anything in the exterior world of physicality create beliefs?]

"Yes."

[What ?]

"People. People can. People in your exterior world can create interior spiritual events. First, in themselves and then in others. Many have done this. This is what you are doing now. That is what all of humanity can do."

[But how ? How can we do this? That is the golden question.]

"There are many ways in which one may begin."

[Name one.]

"You are holding it in your hand."

Here of course, reference was being made to their book. .

This quotation from *Tomorrows God* is included here for this simple reason: I feel that Neale Donald Walsch's publications qualify as extremely valuable reading. His early introductory experiences were somewhat akin to mine. I, however, was spared the almost desperate, lonely lifestyle he underwent. I was eased into the experience of thought plane transference while I was in the company of supportive and trusting friends. Everyone's experience will be different, and no one is denied it. The key? It's simple: get quiet. This will take time and lots of practice; it is not easy. Distractions abound once you step into that room of your life. The recipe also includes a large portion of Intent, and then Allowing must be folded in. Trust is the other ingredient needed. Lots of Trust. You can't add too much Trust.

I encourage the reading of at least the first three chapters of *Tomorrow's God*. Then you be the judge as to whether you read any further. My guess is that you'll make it a "must read."

This manual provides only basic information for each (UIKE)[4] presently occupying its human form. This information is intended to enable any and all to recall and personally achieve pre-selected goals.

This manual is a short version of what could be a 300-page book. Many kind folks have read and critiqued this effort. One primary person is Linda Mae, my physical partner, my friend, my fellow traveler and, in this "go round," my wife. In some ways, Linda was the one who started this whole thing for me, consciously. Linda's many years of accompanying me to fascinating Circle of Light and Universalia meetings also set the scene for many intense conversations at our breakfast table, triggered many times, after little sleep due to all the unbelievable subjects to which we'd been introduced. Each of our days are now spent in more reading, reviewing and yes, more discussions. Along with the quiet time, of course.

It seems to me that, in all situations, there has to be a Most Important Partner. There certainly is ONE in my case; My (Other) Partner. IT is definitely 'the silent type'.

And, interestingly enough, you have The Same Partner with you. Perhaps You choose to call IT by another name. (That's cool.) Or you may be reluctant to even allow IT as a possibility, for whatever reason. (That is, in my opinion, not cool.) Today, many hu-mans admit, however, that this Game is much easier when their Partner is consciously in their corner.

When I use the word "we" I'm referring to The Partner.

You will find interspersed throughout this manual input from The Partner. I promise you that I merely took dictation. Quite often, reading the input after receiving it a day or so previ-

---

[4] Undefinable, Indescribable Kosmic Energy = YOU

ously was as unbelievable to me as it may be for you as you read this.

Just allow.
Allow the content of this manual to be...
a possibility.

Welcome To Our Quiet

The sun shines: I AM. I receive from the great sun as the program calls to receive. The light of the sun gives unto its own that which knows the truth.

The winds give unto the receivers. Carrying all the messages of all the providers of messages to be carried—and I speak unto thee. Though subtle it may appear to be—yet I speak. I like subtlety. It is less noticeable and requires the quick of mind to grasp. I prefer the quiet, the smooth of time. Such scenes provide meshing to take place, such as the meshing of our vibrations at this moment. Quiet is my time. I left it. It was permitted to be in amongst all the other created time users. But instead I left it to be—that this might be. That WE, together—might be.

Expression requires a canvas on which to express. It calls for a gathering point to come to be. The quiet is that place, pregnant with potential, yet needing the focus of intent to bring potential to reality of expression. The quiet is a favorite of MINE in actuality, for it offers such great unknown combinations of expression. Unknown, until the final expression is expressed—be it a work of art, music or expression of conceived word.

Then, once expressed, the value of the quiet is once more known to those who understand the purpose of quiet, the strength in quiet, the truth in quiet.

Welcome again, my son—to our quiet.

"Welcome to our quiet" is a preview. I heartily invite you to step into a new space and be re-introduced to a kosmos of which you have very little (or perhaps - no) recall.

This manual is about a Game and you—both you and the Game—are completely, totally intertwined and interconnected. The Game is an especially unusual game. You could easily call it "the game of a lifetime."

The Game is neither illegal, immoral, nor fattening. However, it does allow any person to realize any and all of those physical world conditions along with their attendant convoy of experiences.

This Game's framework is totally different from any other game known to man. (Its vast size has a lot to do with that.)

NOW –
Do you have the inclination, desire, and ability to think big?

What we're about to disclose is credible, inside information. From this point on in your reading you must be open to what may become for you—remembered truths. The Game we refer to is of cosmic proportions and dimensions therefore, you must be ready, willing, and able to think BIG.

Not Super Bowl Big. Bigger.   The World Olympics?

BIGGER!

The impact of the present computer-Internet explosion is even dwarfed by The Game we are all playing.

What are the rules of The Game?

The Game, interestingly enough, has very few rules. *However,* in accordance with the framework of allowances endemic to it, moving through this Game are many well-meaning "authorities" of certain types. They are playing it, and making up their own rules. They may show up in ones life experiences.

Each player may play The Game wherever the player chooses. How the player plays the game is limited only by the player's beliefs and thoughts. Many books regarding this point are now available—but not to all players. Some are still operating under the allowed coaching of others. (Those "authority figures"). This would be an example and form of being asleep.

Is The Game really able to be "won"?

The Game hides how to win from the players through a devious technique of distractions brought on via man's creativity. A divine dichotomy if ever there was one! And, from the information we're receiving, the game may be winning.
(I suspect The Game may even have a consciousness)

How is it possible that The Game can be winning?

The distractions have been and are, even now, overpowering the players. First the primary distraction was survival, and still is for many. This was followed by tribal controls, expanding into national interests. Next, comfort levels in living the good life became not only a challenge but also a major distraction. The good life has been superseded by man's creative abilities resulting in technologies of all kinds. (Atlantis: all over again?)

Now, the major and huge distraction is the ever-present element within The Game: fear. It is evidenced in its varying faces of greed, hate, and the acceptance of misguided "truths," some of which, as we are witnessing, lie within the guise of religion.

The angst of Christmas is just one example.

The controlling of individual's personal lives *and beliefs* to a point of creating non loving actions in places all around the world; we are witness to daily.

One Ole Guy's Journey

A few years ago I saw a cartoon in which inside the form of an old man is a young man saying, "What the hell happened?" I easily relate to that. I recently celebrated 75 years living in this Game. This manual is the culmination of thirty steady years of study and research—personal research involving a multitude of unusual experiences in unique groups and reading myriad books. I participated in groups of like-minded people for more than twenty years. From those group experiences, we deduced that the paranormal and metaphysical were well worth investigating experientially. Exploring those unsuspected areas opened interests and varied subject matter which allowed me to learn volumes.

Neale Donald Walsch, in *Conversations with God, Book I*, describes his experience of inspired writing. I have experienced similar phenomena, as do many writers. Writings have come to me from Source. Here in this manual, you are privy to some. I trust the sources of my input and gladly share these messages with you. This manual is a sharing. In being open to Source energy, I have been a participant in the knowing, love, and peace available to us all. I have been in the presence of and communicated with souls in transition and have been amazed. Still, I'm just a human participating in The Game. And, for us all, The Game continues.

Please open yourself to information regarding quantum physics, kinesiology, guided meditation, and psychic experiences. *Power vs. Force*, the first book in the David Hawkins trilogy, is just one of many which may further your awakening. I was particularly drawn to the section "About the Author."

Walter Russell's book, *The Secret of Light* was, for me, beautifully stupefying. Here's a short excerpt found on page vii:

> "Man progresses in cycles of approximately twenty-five hundred years. At the beginning of each cycle of his growing awareness of the Light within him, God sends messages through prepared messengers to further his comprehension of the Light. Comprehension of these cosmic messages gradually exalts mankind into higher beings, and thus each cycle is one more step for man toward full awareness of the Light, and of his Oneness with God."

Ken Wilber's *Integral Spirituality* says much of the same thing, only differently, of course.

Equally amazing are the works of Vitvan, a forest ranger who, in the silence of the forests of the northwestern United States, developed the skill of seeing the energy of the trees. His story is a testament to the fact that any ordinary human being, just like you and me, has access to the extraordinary—if we'll just open to the quiet.

During my journey of opening, the saying, "my Father's house has many mansions" took on vast new meaning. More than seven years of delightful and enlightening experiences were a gift I received while participating with Universalia, a unique group in Denver, Colorado. It was there that thought plane transference was introduced to us by our group's guides. All twelve plus Universalia members developed this channeling skill at the behest and with the aid of, probably, our group guides.

A collection of offerings from within this dedicated group soon became more than sufficient material for our bi-monthly newsletter, as recommended by our group's guides. "The Universalian" was mailed by request all over the world. Interestingly enough, that newsletter was supported totally by donation.

The Kyrian Letters by Sandra Radhoff (now Sandra Lund) is a direct result of our Universalia experience. It is a wonderful, enlightening book that can be read many times and still feel fresh. Thanks to Sandy, Kyros, a light being within her entourage, became a steady and loving source of strength and support to all the members of both our group and subscribers to "The Universalian." It is amazing what transpires when one trusts and allows.

The offering below added another piece to this amazing and beautiful journey. In February of 1983, my strong desire to know was mounting in intensity by the day. Quite often I would pose a question at the top of my tablet, get quiet, and await the answer. That time I wrote, "What is your will for me?" Below is just a segment of the channeling that came through. You'll find it in it's entirety on page 95. Personally, I find that it invites multiple readings and much thought.

> *My will for you is to experience. To have the full library of knowing, through personal experience, those areas of growth possibilities which certain planetary workshops have to offer in the way of experience.*

> *My will is for your understanding to be continuous, toward a more complete knowing, which may lead to even further personal awareness, which permits further extension and expansion of the part you represent to the completion of which I AM.*

As I now understand it, "a more complete knowing" definitely involves first *allowing the possibility* of other answers to all questions to be available and then *trusting* that those answers come from a reliable, credible, and loving connection. A practice one may develop and bring about.

I also then came to realize that "for you" in that passage is to be read in the plural, meaning "for all of you." When I first read it, I was so blown away that I thought Source was talking just to me. Not true, as I now understand it.

This has been one growing experience, to say the least!

The Puzzle Just Got Bigger

After many of the Universalia meetings and most of the Friday night Circle of Light meetings, a common exclamation of mine to Linda, as we drove home to Castle Rock was, "Wow! the puzzle just got bigger." Many of our group experiences qualified as mind blowing. In regard to my Ouija board experience, Chelsea Q. Yarbro alludes to a similar set of circumstances, but different of course, in *Messages from Michael*. That Ouija board opened for me, yet another mansion in "my Father's house."

"In my Fathers house are many mansions," indeed!

Another one of those mansions is trance medium work. Although I have done some trance medium work, I find that Ramtha, who is channeled by J.Z. Knight, to be a particularly interesting personality. Ramtha's message is now routinely reintroduced by others and seldom improved upon.

Along the way, I was also introduced to yet another aspect of Source. This one was of a slightly different type than Ramtha. It was a "collective being" called Amag, presenting "themselves" through an unassuming young woman from Montana. At the Colorado University hospital auditorium in Denver, this amazing trance medium displayed the uncanny ability to speak and write quite legibly on a clean flip chart with her eyes closed. Although a good deal more could be said about Amag, I interject here a short offering from Them.

> *"We are a multiplicity of individuality, representative of the wisdom of SOURCE. Wisdom of the awareness of SOURCE. What is that 'multiplicity? Multiple, many individual repre-*

sentatives of the unity of SOURCE. And then, so are all of you—many individual representatives of the unity of SOURCE."

All these beings are aspects of Source—Ramtha, Amag, me, and you—all different. One of the keys is how well we listen and what we choose to hear.

Really: It's a Kosmic Game

The Essence of The Game

When we stop and look around this world, we see that Earth is overflowing with games. Games are played anywhere and everywhere on this planet—on tables, in sandlots, on sidewalks, in the backyard, in the vacant lot, and at the park. People worldwide play games in which they ride animals and manipulate objects of every shape, size, and description. They drive wheeled vehicles around, over, and past objects indescribable. It boggles the mind the number of marathon runners doing their thing on any given day everywhere in the world. And it is staggering to see the impact of soccer, football, baseball, tennis, and cricket on the lives of humans everywhere. Even the concept of survival itself has been turned into a game on TV! ("As below, so above ?" . . . . I think so.)

We must not overlook the contests of poker, bridge, chess, ping pong, go, mahjong, and dominos worldwide. Not to be outdone, of course, are the games of chance. These may, in truth, be the most popular if we could track the total number of players. Yes, worldwide "the game is the thing" for billions of people. And we didn't even mention video games, did we? As above, so below and vice versa—it's possible!

Why, it's as if even Source loves games!

And now that we're in planet-wide thinking mode, you are invited to expand your perspective and think even bigger.

Think BIG – Really … BIG.

Now – think outside

and beyond

that.

Think : Planets as locations for Games!

Life on Earth is a game of Kosmic dimensions, and once one moves into that framework, it is easy to consider that this is probably not the only game around.Definitely designed by Masters, its parameters are, of course, totally different from any and all games on Earth.
…and, we could easily say, "not in a league with."

Every person on this planet ventured voluntarily onto this game board known as Earth. You are all participating in a kosmic game designed for soul-framed energies. Humans: being and doing—to experience. It is our intention that this manual will supply the answers to questions such as, What's with this place called Earth?

You are one with Source, God, or whatever you call your Creator. You and the entire company of actors whom you observe daily continue to create the sets, the backdrops, and the environment; virtually everything pertaining to this theatre in the spherical. This makes the inhabitants of this planet (you) celestial beings! And, [now get this!], in comparison to what you truly are, this whole game board/stage on which you are playing is an illusion—a kosmic illusion. Walter Russell alludes to it in Chapter XV in *The Secret of Light*.

Many are asking, "Why am I here?"

Some of you came here to aid in the kosmic process.

This being all in accordance with your blueprint.

Others may stay with The Game until they win, and some have been caught up in a seemingly involuntary series of re-entries.

Others of you won previously and, no doubt have returned to assist both the planet and its inhabitants. Again, you are each functioning according to your blueprint.

The Game offers unlimited options. Souls have been experi-
encing it for unbelievable centuries. It is a challenging place.
It provides thrills and chills and spills and all that goes with
those activities. As a cosmic theatre, it provides vast costume
changes and even more vast backdrops. It provides opportuni-
ties for beautifully divine and completely unsavory character
parts. Thus its appeal.

Although it may be difficult for some of you to allow this idea,
the background and entire premise for this manual is celestial, even more celestial than *Star Wars*. It's simple: the real
'me' doesn't need a space ship.

There is a valid reason for that, too. This is a manual about us
hu-mans—"hue," as in light through prisms and rainbows, and
"man," as in all the folks we see on TV, on the street, at the
airport, at work, at church, in the gym, at school, across the
street, and across the table—even in the mirror.

We are celestial. It's hard to believe, but we came from the
stars.

"Nonsense!" you say?

Oh, you have forgotten!

You are more than the colors of the season, the rainbows in the sky and its accompanying bold light displays. Your essence is merely in a covered-over state lying and waiting to be uncloaked. To be given air to breathe and grow more fully toward the True LIGHT of its being—LIGHT glowing deep, solid, sure and forever, awaiting rekindling of its True Nature.

This manual re-introduces you to a Game so phenomenal that those playing it don't even recall that they are in this Game.

Yes, dear Reader, you have forgotten. You have forgotten many key, yet unrecognized factors within this Game called Life on Earth. These include:

- You have forgotten what you are.

- You have forgotten why you chose to get involved at this point in the planet's evolutionary cycle.

- You have forgotten how to win The Game; and this factor is **vitally important to both the planet and all the players.** (I've not alluded to the factor of mass consciousness—have I? We've left that for another edition.)

Here Are the Notes You Didn't Bring

Most games are contests in which the players attempt to outlast, outrun, outguess, outsmart, and ultimately outscore everyone else in the contest. The goal is to win. Only one of those points has anything to do with this Game—the key goal: to win.

Every game, this one included, has guidelines that become obvious to anyone who intends to win. They include:

- Enjoy the game.
- Understand the rules; study the game.
- Practice diligently and regularly.
- Create a mindset to win
- Focus on winning.

This is not a rule book. This manual is to help re-introduce you to a reality of which you have very little recall. If you and others did, this world would be an entirely different place. This manual is a compilation of perceived factors which relate to (a) the planet and its kosmic relationship to the billions of human inhabitants and (b) what those inhabitants in essence are. Those two factors combine to create an astounding format for experiencing.

The Game is rife with unsuspected elements; *illusion* for one. Illusion, of course, from a Kosmic perspective. Kosmic being the underlying source, premise, and framework for every concept in this manual.

CAUTION: Due to dogmatic rules allowed within the experience of most humans, you may have difficulty accepting these ideas.

RECOMMENDATION: Take what you can, and set the rest aside. During your reading of this manual or upon its completion, a spark, a light that has been only glowing softly in that secret place within your Temple of Life may be fanned to brilliance. That is what this manual is intended to do. Why? The probability is that millions of souls are awakening to their true nature: Divinity.

OUR purpose for this manual is to assist YOU to be as completely aware of your Divinity as possible and it applies, of course, **to all people** living upon this planet.

It's an Image Thing

Most human beings have some idea of a Greater Power, God, or Being, or whatever. Here, we refer to it as Source. I certainly admit, there is something far greater in all ways than what I see myself to be. Why? Because we know we sure can't and didn't consciously create those wonderful sunsets, those beautiful flowers, and certainly not the joy-filled presence of a newborn....anything.

According to "The Good Book," we are made in His image. Why does it say that? Simple. The reference to "He" and "His" easily came as a result of the people who translated all those writings, scrolls of papers, which finally became the Holy Scriptures.
Theirs was a patriarchal society. For the most part, men were doing or overseeing the translations, so naturally, anything so powerful had to be a "He." If you're not sure what I mean, think of the Sistine chapel: There's God, gray haired with a pretty good-looking (human) body wrapped in a sheet, and He touches his finger to Adam (another guy) to give him life and power. Great art!

This manual will be easier to understand—and to accept — with a small adjustment in semantics and will definitely be more acceptable to the female 50 percent of the population if the word referencing that "image" is reconfigured, so to speak.

Let's agree to move from a human image orientation to one of energy. "God is Love" is a well-accepted way of thinking about Source as energy rather than matter.

(LOVE) "seeks to damage or hurt no one. It seeks to avoid the possibility of damage or hurt to anyone."[5]

Love or Source is positive power in every sense of the word. Matters will be simplified for these few moments or days, depending on how long you are immersed in this reading, if you will accept this shift in semantics. The God (or Source of All That Is) that you and I know (down deep) cannot be the kind of "he" in all that great art.

Energy is the basis for the system in which we move, breathe, and love. Quantum physics has, for most of us, clarified this. A good place to start is *The Holographic Universe* by Talbot, which explains much about quantum physics in layman's terms. Thus, kosmic energy will be our basis for this manual. Myriad studies and experiments regarding energy are available to us. Walter Russell's *The Secret of Light* is another excellent source of information.

Energy is man's kosmic (and natural) image.

The kosmic energy we're referring to is better defined as agape (pronounced ah-gop-eh), a Greek word for unconditional love which is, (as my Grandma Tucker used to say when I would visit her out in western Kansas), "a far cry" from the Hollywood type of love.

---

[5] Neale Donald Walsch, *Friendship With God*

Agape love beautifully frames all of LIFE. We just don't see it with our eyes. One way we are able to "see" that we are kosmic energy is through our auras. Perhaps you have heard of people who see auras, the emotional energy field generated by every living being. To see it is a fascinating ability. You can even train yourself to see auras. I know several people who see auras; you might see them, too without realizing what you just saw. Perhaps you saw a color around someone's head. In the ancient paintings of holy people, the halo was most likely their aura, which was very bright, bright enough for many to see.

"It (aura) is a miniaturization of a hologram of us, complete with DNA structure, attitudes, our belief system; all we assume to be us. Our fields extend out 6 inches to a foot beyond our physical body."[6]

So, if energy is primary and basic to this place we call Earth, and if we are kosmic energy, then what do we look like?

When we try to see electricity, it's invisible. Under the right circumstances, however, we can certainly feel its presence. Think of walking into a home where love and respect are abundant, the "energy" (or vibes) is evident when you pause and allow it to surround you. Conversely, when we enter into a room where a fight has just taken place, negative vibrations are detectable. It's in the air. There you have it. "Image" has now taken on a different look (pun intended).

Since the energy in question isn't readily seen, it would be more helpful to clarify what you in the human body on Earth are not. You are not your body. Well, you are, and you're not. It depends on what your definition of "are" is.

You/we are the kosmic energy supply for, designer of, and, to some extent, the caretaker of the body/form/vehicle in which we move, sense, and have our experiences.

---

[6] Sheradon Bryce, *Joyriding the Universe*.

"But wait!" I can hear you saying, "aren't we made in the image of God?" With words, man has for centuries attempted to define what God is. I contend—with words—man cannot even begin to define or describe Source. There are no words in existence to define or describe Source.

Think about it:

The
Source
of All
That Is

The Alpha and The Omega

The

Tao

"The Tao that can be spoken is not the Eternal Tao"

Creator

of

Heaven

and

Earth

That's about as close as one can come to describing or naming IT

<u>VERY IMPORTANT</u> ! Remember, although we all are "just" aspects, we are still "bona fide members of the firm," in *every sense of the word.*

Joined at the heart.

Eternally.

<u>Everyone</u> has the "company" of The Partner.

Source silently "stands at the door" waiting until the connection is sought (intent) and allowed (focus) *by us*. That connection is always on.

What's the hook? It requires intent, which must be paired with focus.

Both those attitudes must come from us.

However, and I don't have to point this out …..The Game is continuously throwing distractions at us.

Your neighbors, your "brothers and sisters" are kosmic energy, just as you are. You/we see them as humans, however. You will agree, I'm sure, that the human body is amazing. The equipment within it—eyes, brain, lungs, blood, and all the rest – it is phenomenal! The planning and preparation that went into the human body is totally breathtaking! Included in it is a mental/emotional package, which combines with the physical package to produce perceptions that are individual and personal—your very own.

And the coup de grace is that the spirit/unit of consciousness that is using the body assists in providing the body kosmic energy and may give *healing* if allowed. The human form is the vehicle of choice, having been designed specifically to grow and change, thus enabling us to experience life while living on Earth. By doing so, we may know, according to our perceptions what it is like to be here.

The human form is also designed to enable Source of this indescribably awesome planetary workshop to know of ITSELF according to each of IT's aspect's (that is us: yours and my) perceptions. Along with that, the body provides you/us with the ability to experience the planet consciously. Every human form on this planet is consciousness. Think about it. You know, and you know that you know what you know. But what you truly know is only what you have experienced. And you know that from your own unique perspective. Any and everything else is myth. It is someone else's experience and their allowed knowledge all shared with you/us by word of mouth, print, or imagery from which we draw our own perceptions—and at times—erroneously.

All the experiences that you and all other humans on Earth are having right now are experienced right along with you by Source.

That is why you/they/we are here. We are all experiencing. That's not difficult to understand and accept. However, for some the jury is still out as to whether or not we are chauffeuring Source around with us (even in a small sense). Due to earlier training, many think, "He's out there"- somewhere. But (think about it), we are probably providing the only means available for Source to have feedback on what Source created, from the most minute to the most immense. You support the activity of the form in which you function while on Earth— the human body. You are directly associated with the computer brain while operating within this Game. You assimilate in myriad ways all those multitudinous sensations the body enables via all its sensory technology. Source also intakes those feelings, experiences, and sensations as well—simultaneously, instantly. That's right! All your sensations, every thought, wish, fear: all input is received by Source simultaneously and <u>unconditionally.</u> That means totally without judgment. Source takes in each and every experience, be it grandiose or mundane.

What does that mean?

That means we Two are One and the same Energy. The One Source is just <u>far more powerful</u> than is our kosmic energy. As a result of this co-arrangement, Source is able to know of ITs potential as Provider and Co-creator.

We usually see ourselves in the driver's seat of this vehicle. But by really allowing our Source to be a participant in The Game in a very close, real, and quiet manner, that puts Source in the entire front seat. Just imagine that scenario….Source is "riding shotgun!" well, sort of. Don't you love it! And so few of us take advantage of IT.

Example: you go out snorkeling with friends. You experience the ocean as you dive and swim through it. Obviously, that little bit of contact with the ocean is your very own (but not) unique experience. Thus, you know of the ocean to a minute degree, only. Each of your friends also knows the ocean to their own minute degree, and their experiences are slightly different than your experience of it. If you had the ability to "plug into" their perceptions, emotions and experiences just as they experienced the ocean and *know* it the very same way they did, then you could experience it all in addition to your own. Just imagine that indescribable event! I admit: I can't.

Source has that grand opportunity moment by moment. Source is literally with you/us/everyone every moment; every experience by great (*or otherwise*) experience, thought by thought, emotion by emotion.

The major problem within this human condition is:
Most everyone has forgotten their relationship to Source.
Fortunately, there are some units of consciousness, in human
form of course, presently on the planet for the sole purpose to
maintain balance. Their presence is assisting in offsetting the
violence and fear being promulgated by those who have no
idea of who they are and in this lifetime may never catch a
clue.

There is an effort "afoot" to attach some allowing onto those
folks. We see it almost everyday now in the most unsuspecting places and from the most unsuspecting sources. People,
of course speaking their piece (peace) as they are "brought to
do". It's truly wonderful to observe.

What You Have Forgotten

Most of us—including the street person, cabbie, banker, salesman, policeman, artist, laborer, housewife, race driver, architect, broker, bus driver, bag lady, business owner, camel driver, chiropractor, caddie, fireman, farmer, truck driver, student, dentist, printer, retired person, millionaire, billionaire, motorcyclist, mother, terrorist, bicyclist, iron worker, new bride, dog groomer, entertainer, egg rancher, teacher, train conductor, orchestra conductor and all the rest—have forgotten. Forgotten the most beautiful part of this life.

Drink these pages in very, very slowly. Here is the first of only a few truths about You. To be fair; this first one—you have not forgotten. You have just been so distracted and busy that you haven't bothered to take this into consideration as being a divine quality.

You (and everyone else) are each

a Unit of Consciousness.

This divine gift stands on its own. It is an unmatched quality within creation. Consciousness is so taken for granted, it is totally overlooked. The players see not its basic beauty as a gift from the Creator. You are an indestructible, incredible, and complete Unit of Consciousness functioning in a place where the human form is in vogue (and it too, is an illusion).Where you came from you are free of limitations of movement. Remember, you are real, a free "form."

You "AM" just as Source is "I AM."

"Man is the only unit in creation who has *conscious awareness* of the spirit within him and *electrical awareness* of dually conditioned light acting upon his senses."[7]

---

[7] Walter Russell, *The Secret of Light*

Reflections on The Pond
Consciousness: The endless rippling Pond reflecting its own Light—Science and Truth; Nuclei and Ovum; there is but To Be. Like Droplets among droplets, Seas among seas, Worlds beyond worlds. Timelessly, each pearl passes through the endless membranes—simply To Become. Invisible forces transform us, excite us, Become us. Back and forth, in and out—we continue to Glisten—a tiny fragment of Eternal light. The Pond: One Body (Divine)—yet, each Droplet Reflects unto its very Source, forevermore. –TD

You had and have the freedom to express in whatever manner you choose, on whatever planetary stage in any galaxy. You chose this particular planet, for it enables you to know the feelings of success at overcoming the myriad challenges specific to this planetary experience, this Kosmic Game.

A major challenge to most Units of Consciousness was (and is, for as you notice, they're continuing to be born) the inability to recall *what you really are* while in this Game. Such a concept is totally foreign to an **Eternal Unit of Consciousness** that knows what it is. It cannot fathom being something that does not know what it is. It seems incredulous.

Yet, such is the case with this Game. It removes your recall as to what You really are upon entry (i.e., birth) into The Game. The actual way this memory removal takes place is immaterial (and we would probably not understand it anyhow). But the challenge remains; we're here.

After all, everyone has to be somewhere, right? Right. And in order to win this Game, we must consciously recall our true nature and live according to who we really are. That means not just a mental "OK" kind of acceptance, but an actual **conscious experience** of being one with Source before we leave The Game. In other words, we had best arrive at that game-winning-point of awareness before we remove ourselves from this Game (i.e., before we "die"). Those qualifications are all in alignment with our blueprint.

Where You came from You are a free form—there's a paradox for you. Free of limitations of movement. For the True You, the confining characteristics of both the human body and the imposed boundaries of The Game are, needless to say, constraining and limiting **to the extreme**.

The planning that takes place prior to ones entry into The Game is inscribed onto a blueprint that is ever with us, carried by our soul. It is available for our review, should we care to refer to it. Most players, however, are so distracted by the glitter and glamour of this game that they simply don't bother to take the time to reflect before making a choice, to check in with the blueprint. And that's okay; it is just one of many options one is presented throughout the game. A big one, obviously. And, you know what? The Game sees to that.

Do you want to win this Kosmic Game? If so, here's one way how:

*(Not recommended while driving a car or operating machinery.)

Sit easily in a quiet place.

Observe your breath closely and intentionally.

Disregard all else. Eyes closed; helps.

Breathe more deeply than normal, quiet the mental chatter.

Take control of the process consciously.

Don't worry—You've got time.

The Consciousness which is You is not at all unique unto You. However, the multitude of experiences within your library are most definitely unique to you (and known by Source, of course) at this point in your growth.

"The decision-making process is a function of consciousness itself; with enormous rapidity, the mind makes choices based on millions of pieces of data and their correlations and projections, far beyond conscious comprehension."

—Dr. David Hawkins, *Power vs Force*

"We must remain open to all of these possibilities. In a universe that is conscious right down to its very depths, animal, plants, even matter itself may all be participating in the creation of these phenomena."

— Michael Talbot, *The Holographic Universe*.

This page is for you to write your thoughts and your feelings after getting quiet and observing your breath. Come back in three days and read this page. Keep seeking the quiet.

Did you see colors?

Source is with me at all times?

I planned to be here? (answer any feelings?)

Déjà vu feelings or experiences you recall?

You are Kosmic Energy—
electromagnetic by nature.

Source desired to experience as fully as possible all that had been created. However, the inherent power within Source precluded ITs ability to focus on anything. ITs kosmic power required a "stepping down" or reducing of that power. (The transformer on the light pole does a similar process.) Source, in order to focus on anything, had to create a *means through which* that focusing could take place, so voila! The Divine sparks began to fly. The result: introduction of Divine Aspects of THE ALL. a.k.a (also known as) "**Children of God.**" Aspects of Source—which have the same creative bent, same humor, same consciousness, same everything as Source, except for one difference: those children/aspects were a lesser degree of kosmic energy volume. As a result and *in keeping with the plan*, all aspects were allowed, yes—even encouraged to go, do, and be anywhere and everywhere ... for Source.

The Law
The Law of Universal Attraction dominates discussion in recent time. Divine Sparks. You are Kosmic Energy. Electromagnetic. Like Beings. Like thoughts. Like attracts Like. All—initiated with— thought. –TD

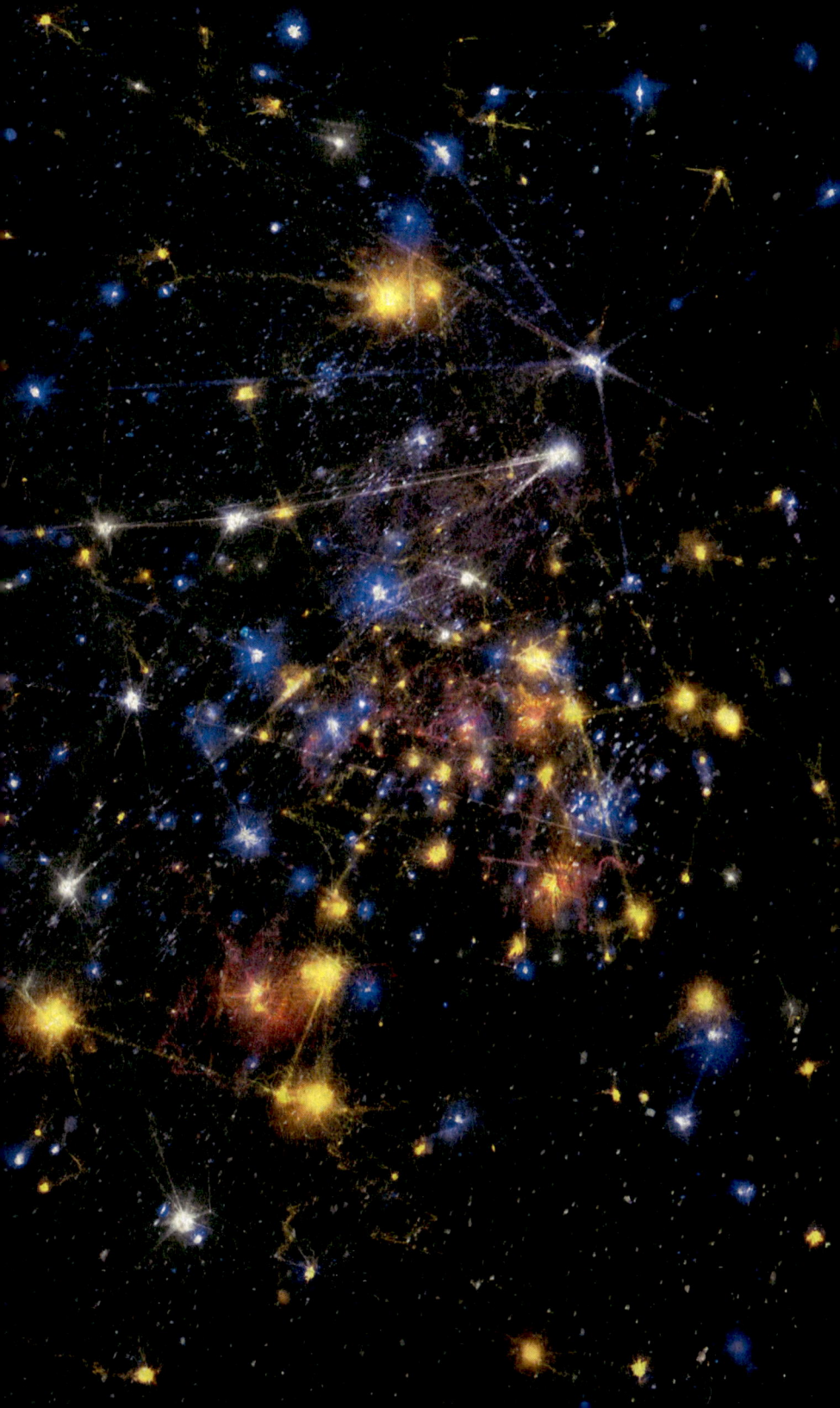

"Never forget Who You Are! You are IT ALL. You are not limitation. You are not a confused mistake. You are a vast, brilliant, extending, creative energy field that exploded out of the Heart of the ONE and is delighting in its journey Home. Remember ... please Who You Are."[8]

> *Energy knows no bounds. You have witnessed that. When given proper conditions energy must be expressed. That is the law. Continue in the development of your quiet connection. It will come to be a lifesaver for many, actually. For as the awakening wave commences to gain momentum there will be those who are having the feelings of awakening who will be gathered in to the wave itself ...thus the momentous swell of love will be given its 'go ahead' signal.*

> *"And the last will truly become—the first"*

So you still think there are coincidences? No! It's all in the magnetics between (a) you, (b) the human form, and (c) The Game. Being electromagnetic is another wondrous quality regularly used by man, although the "spectators" of this Game might say, 'rather poorly at times.'

Electromagnetic kosmic energy is an integral element all humans take advantage of (or) feel its negative results throughout all their experiences in The Game.

---

[8] Bartholomew, *From the Heart of a Gentle Brother*

This page is for your observations regarding recent coincidences.

Did you consciously call in the situation? Have you ever? Why not set one up? After all, you have the ability. Try it on clouds, for starters.

Where is your trust level? Why? Because you are writing your own script. Do you believe that? Analyze your trust levels this past month.

If not, why not?

Return to this page in 7, 15, then 30 days.

Think about this to a point of remembering.

That is done only in quiet time.

Source is Love and You are Love.

YOU are functioning as Love Incarnate,
Love in human form.
Yes, here you are, along with all those "others"
confined in a dense form—compared to the real YOU.

Taking all that into consideration, such a set of circumstances
can be daunting. It is time to remember: trust and allow that
YOU were created out of Love
YOU were created by Love
YOU will always Be…It.

YOU know this. Now, you understand that tug on your
heartstrings when you hear of someone's hard times, or abuse,
or receipt of any other non-loving act.

**It is time, now, for you to know
the truth of YOUR being.
How?
Take time – quiet time.**

Flight of Love By Love—Seeking Love
Knowing Truth, the Music of the Spheres draws us nearer. We are
here—but We are there. The Journey is both endless and finite.
Rainbows of Emotion. Orbs of Passion. Cells of Mystery uniting
Energy and Matter in Living Free-form without limit. We are Birds
of Joy seeking Light in The Celebration of Existence and Timeless
Unity. –T. Donahue ("and Love from…out there.")

YOU are love—manifesting.
Your body is love—manifested/manifesting.
Your planet home is love—manifesting/manifested.
Your fellow man is love reflecting unto YOU your (perceived)
imperfection state as a student in the school of truth. This is also
an expression of love, provided for your individual, unique growth.
As people are given opportunities to freely interact with each other,
thence they become more aware of that bond of love between
themselves and their mutual connection with Source.
Once realized through experience it is forever owned.
Since the day of your creation you have been seeking the reality of
freedom through experience—freedom in its many aspects:
personal, individual, group, national, and planetary.
As you can see they are many. They are many faceted and will
require many, many experiential situations to supply a full
understanding to be realized (if ever), for freedom brings with it
many opportunities for expression.
Others might say, "and responsibilities."
The place, gap, or opening between freedom to do nothing and
anything is vast, almost like a vacuum. Filling it, however, may
become a challenge when one is shackled with fears, frustrations,
and limiting beliefs.

You are hereby invited to shed the cape of fear.

NOW.

Place your thoughts here, just for you to see.

What does Love feel like to you NOW?

When you see a simple flower—do you see Love?

How is fear holding you?

You are invited to—In your naked feet—walk slowly in the grass, sand, or carpet.

–Breathe more deeply than you have ever breathed before.

(What colors do you notice?)

You are Eternal.

Eternal?
But of course.

It would follow quite naturally:

> ENERGY is
> LOVE is
> YOU is
> ETERNAL.

(Our apologies to all English teachers everywhere.)

Have fun in your quiet time
wrapping your mind around all this.

Take time, now.
Listen to the quiet of a candle glow.
Hear its heart and joy.
Listen to the quiet.
See the Joy in the light of the Moon.
Hear it.
"Be" in quiet.

Soul Riders
Ancient-Modern Energies. The endless horizon of Time is the abode of the Soul as IT glides with It's Heart-Treasure called "Life". Undaunted. Fearless. Existing of ITS own Light. Without Limit. Dimension-less. A Beauty Eternal. –TD

Life is a happening. It is always happening. It is an ongoing, forward event, for such is Its nature. Life on Earth flows continuously; all the while appearing to change. IT is LIFE.

YOU support in many ways the activity of the form in which you function while on Earth, i.e., the human body. Each YOU is aligned with the computer brain located in the head of the body as it is functioning within The Game. The body is so designed with varied and myriad sensory equipment built into its make-up; perceptions thus become one's basis of truth. Your truth is based on previous input. All the while you are consciously aware, YOU draw to you those multitudinous sensations. And YOU know this.

Source of All That Is also intakes those feelings as well. Simultaneously. Instantly. All your sensations, all your thoughts. All input is received by Source simultaneously and unconditionally. This means totally without judgment.

All humans are just like YOU.
And, almost all humans have forgotten.

How are you doing on that quiet time?
We didn't say it was easy;
We said it was simple.
Stay with it, now.

Meditating twice a day is good.
First thing after bidding hello to the sun.

(Sounds silly—doesn't it?) But that'll be OK no one is watching nor listening. That would be after You've assured you that YOU love you while looking deep into your eyes in the mirror.

It's time your daily habits took a different path since you're desiring different results.

Write down what those different results might be—it's OK if you add more pages here. This is a manual—remember.

The second time to meditate is when you can get to a really quiet place—express your gratitude for your life experience and get really quiet—again. A background tape or CD might be useful.

You are also........

Beauteous Light

"For to thee I again say, all things are Light,
and Light separates not; nor has it bounds:
nor is it here and not there."
And as the rainbow is a light within the Light, inseparable,
so is Man's Self within Me inseparable,
and so is his image My image."[9]

You are participating in both a carefully designed process and a kosmic challenge: the process of LIGHT functioning in human form. SOURCE desired to be able to experience as fully as possible all that had been created, and IT knew there was to be more. It all was just the beginning.

Daily quiet time is "where IT's at." Find out for yourself. Source is waiting. You are Light in human form strictly for the purpose of experiencing this Earthly workshop in relationships. It's not available anywhere else.

---

[9] Walter Russell, *The Secret of Light* – "The Divine Illiad"

Hannah's Space – the Soular Connections
I am Honored. This painting "Came to Me" in a period of hours through a tiny silent voice. Guidance. Respect. Love. Un-Ending Patience. Motherly Love from a Child-Spirit plus A Willing Scribe: given the Goal of Great Importance. There can be no other way to explain how this Image emerged. –TD

"Man may weave the pattern of his Self in Light of ME, and of his image in divided Lights of ME, e'en as the sun sets up its bow of many hues from divided Light of ME, but man cannot be apart from the Light of ME, as the spectrum cannot be a part of the Light of ME. And as the rainbow is a light within the Light, inseparable, so is Man's self within ME, inseparable, and so is his image MY Image."[10]

The opposite of LIGHT is shadow and darkness of varying degree. The challenge of the game is to infuse the Game with Light which you ARE. Introduce your Light to such a degree it ignites those who are seemingly asleep. This is, of course done with intention. It requires focus. It is not invasive into others' spaces. It is a loving attitude which is prevalent within Soul's space of being as it travels about the planet Earth.

Just as diseases are contagious, so is the Light of the I AM; even more so, for IT is infused with LOVE. The Light of which You are overcomes all negative, fear-filled spaces; therefore, come to know who and what you really are.

"Physical light is not the Light of your soul. Physical light travels at a certain velocity. It cannot go faster. The Light of your soul is instantaneous."[11]

---

[10] W. Russell, The Message of the Divine Iliad, *in Secret of Light*

[11] Gary Zukav in *Seat of the Soul.*

Write down any thoughts coming to you as YOU read this.

Get really quiet, then focus on your heart.

Do it again. Get really quiet, then focus on your heart.

And again. Focus on your heart after getting really, really quiet.

Now, with a single light on any illustrations here, listen to some quiet flute, violin, organ, or piano music.

And since all those qualities qualify as Divine, this makes you and all your peers…

Divine Light

And now we understand those words, "Inasmuch as ye have done it to one of the least of these, so have ye done it unto ME."

"We rest our case" might be our closing remarks if we were closing or arguing for this.
We are, however, doing neither. You know this is how it is.

Seek quiet time…
allowing you to grow into the Beauty.

Within.

Divine Light (The Voice)
Even through Chaos, It Speaks. It Comes from Everywhere—from Nowhere. Without Effort, Erasing Pain. "We are Family: There is Peace." Find the Quiet. Listen to the Universe. –TD

Being Close

Being close is a gift
and in some cases a challenge.
Being close as your heartbeat is also present within the very
breath of your presence.

Merely acknowledge ME.
There is no "how." It is simple. Merely acknowledge ME.

I truly stand at the door and knock.

Quietly, of course—for that is MY style as set by the parameters
of your/our workshop Earth.

Love is the quality of MY force and may be yours once you make
the connection.

To make it—is to know it—is to embrace it unconditionally.
Love is an emotion or feeling, seldom known—due to the inability
to recognize it. Once fully recognized, it is embraced
unconditionally and becomes the criteria for anyone's
actions and thoughts.
Come into the resting place.
Come to know its power.
Recognize distractions for what they are.
Be ready to discard them all. There shall be many.

Remain in focus.

Take some time to think and write about those words and images.

Consider what allowing really means.

Picture you resting in the most tranquil setting you can imagine. Be there. Set any thoughts aside on a shelf just for them, then seek (allow) yourself to know the joy of quiet. What do you feel, see, and hear? Nothing yet? that's OK stay with it... allow yourself time to get "there". After all you've been years getting "here".

It is recommended that you focus on this section of the manual in your regular quiet time. Allow it to penetrate your very being. Remember, you have forgotten what you really are.

> *"As always, my will is for you to know freedom. To know the freedom of Being. To know Being Free—what it has to offer in open freedom qualities and illusionary freedom aspects.*

> *"My will is that you grow into full awareness of your potential and the beauty within that potential as it relates to all 'others' in other worlds and kingdoms, and the empowering which may take place as a result of that awareness as to beauty.*

> *"There is a certain quality unsuspected by those in the human condition that is inherent in the beauty of which I speak. It is impossible to describe, only to be realized, embraced, and used as further strengthening—on—to whatever next level you choose to experience."*

Why does mankind avoid the "now"?

> *Many seek to escape their "is-ness" by immersing themselves in a fascination with past lives and past civilizations. Many seek to escape unto a future of speculation and anticipation of a 'salvation' to come.*
> *But JOY, the rapture of BEING or the presence of SOURCE does not lie in some future.*

> *Others seek escape from what they describe as an illusionary terrestrial reality to take up residence in what they will find to be an equally illusionary astral reality.*
> *All the while they struggle so, they proclaim that which they fail to grasp—that there is no past, no future, no time, no place. There is only the now.*

True JOY, true BEING is immediate, is infinite, is here, is there, is within and is without.

Be still and hear IT.

Be alert and see IT.

Be still and know IT.

Feel IT.

Wonder at IT.

Where is JOY to be found? In the NOW. In the "is-ness" of ALL. In the glory of the stars. In the elegant structure of the onion. In the laugh of any child, the embrace of another—the surge of the wind. JOY may be found in the sea of life and love surrounding all of mankind.

Embrace the moment totally—go into the quiet place. ALL awaits.

(author unknown)

"Today—for one hour—talk not of your past, not even of yesterday, nor say nothing regarding your future—not of tomorrow or even—later today. This will tell you where you are spending your time."[12]

---

[12] Bartholomew, in *from the heart of a gentle brother*.

Now...... About: "Winning"

The following five elements must be known by all players expecting to win The Game. These factors pertain to the relationship between the vehicle and the player, along with the complexity of The Game itself.

1. A pseudo force has been allowed (by you) to be in control of your decisions. That pseudo force is a significant element within your makeup as you go about playing The Game. Likened to an automatic pilot on an airplane, in one sense it is lazy. In many circumstances in your past you have allowed it to determine your actions. It follows habitual thought and practices (wreaking havoc for you due perhaps, to inappropriate use of the Law of Attraction). It routinely pulls from other input (mass consciousness and emotional responses to name only two), thus making life difficult for many players. Changing behavior goes counter to its formatting.

This pseudo force seems to be attracted to all the glitter and glamour of The Game. It hungrily and busily responds to the stimuli of The Game, disallowing any awareness as to what you really are and what your blueprint reads. The force we refer to could be considered ego or personality (and some use other names). Labeling it is difficult due to semantics. This pseudo force (if allowed) takes precedence because YOU (i.e., your soul energy) are not pushy. The Game relies on that fact.

YOU know of course, YOU are the major power behind any of your positive behavior change. That pseudo power just has you thinking it holds the power.

2. Others' beliefs have been allowed (by you) to penetrate and color your perceptions throughout The Game, from the outset. This situation holds true especially when you are the subject. The reason is because the matter of control has run amok within this Game, which is also a workshop of relationships. This control commences for most players at their entry into the workshop (birth) and continues throughout their life. Many parents seek to control their children, most teachers their students, and most employers their employees. Religious leaders even seek to control their followers! The strange thing is–most folks allow it–unless and until the soul moves into the pilot position and changes those settings on allowances. The reason? You have also forgotten the positive freedom framework from whence you came. (reread "What Is Your Will for Me," p. 95)

Allowing remains a key element in the overall formula within The Game. The free-will factor embraces the beauty of allowing. Your clear and thorough understanding of this will be critical.

3. The ever-present negative energy of The Game has been allowed to freely impact your decisions (up to now).

4. Non-credible judgments have been allowed to enter into your perceptions. These come from friends, relatives, peers, family members, coaches, and teachers, to name a few.

5. Input from specific agenda sources, such as the media, has been allowed and continually distracts you from your blueprint.

These and other allowances combine to make this Game one tough challenge. We refer to it as a "workshop" because people seemingly work at it until they get it right. You will be aided greatly if you analyze the above points in light of your life.

After objective evaluation of your personal picture you are encouraged to come to an awareness of what no longer serves you in the field of "allowing." You will benefit immensely if you understand, not just what you really are, but also

a. The power of your thoughts.
b. The law of attraction. (See books by Jerry & Esther Hicks)
c. The true power of each now moment. (See books by Eckhart Tolle)
d. The key to positive allowing.

These critical factors all assist in your balance and provide an increasing awareness of what you really are. Your winning The Game can be the result.

Being discerning now must become the watchword in winning The Game. Being present. Being aware of your thoughts from this point on will be the determinant to winning The Game.

Just remember, you have forgotten from whence you came. You have forgotten that you are Love. You have forgotten that you are Light and Energy of a magnitude indescribable. You have forgotten that you are Eternal. You don't recall that you are far, far more than that physical human body, a fantastic vehicle provided for you to discover the vast challenges of this workshop. You have forgotten that you are Beauty. You have forgotten that you are Consciousness. You have forgotten that you chose to enter this Game rather than other games throughout the kosmos.

And you entered the Game to Win.

In the briefing prior to your birth, you were warned of the deceitful capability of man and the illusionary quality of The Game. Your guides impressed upon you of those two factors, but they have been lost amid the glitter and glamour of The Game; and it has taken its toll: you have forgotten. Consequently, it is natural that you ask, as if in unison, "Why am I here?" "Who am I?" "What is my purpose?" Because it is time. It is time for hundreds, thousands, millions of souls to awaken totally as to What They Really Are.

It is time to wake up and remember.

There is prevalent upon the planet a definite condition of distractions to excess. As a result, a threat to your freedom along with the alignment with *Universal plans for growth* (on many levels) has become a major concern.

A basic element of the game is free will, which can be seen as a two-edged sword. One may do whatever one chooses, all in the frame of reference of free will. However, you also have the freedom to re-connect with your/our Partner and play The Game with guidance from Source.

For many, this game has turned out to be an exercise in doing only that which one desires. Purpose in life seems to have no bearing on one's actions. Instead, the result turns out to be according to someone else's guidance or "living my life my way" all the way.

A beautiful quality prevalent within The Game, however, allows one to choose to totally join with one's Partner and experience this Game openly with Source. Many people in history have done this. They were on the playing field but not in The Game. And they came to know that:

> "Man must know that his power lies in the stillness of his centering self."[13]

---

[13] W. Russell

Allow and participate in quiet time. It's simple, but not easy. The goal of quiet time is to develop the skill of getting truly, completely quiet.

Some who practice meditation regularly commence their session by visualizing a beautiful golden white crystal tent over them. Some use quiet flute, harp, or other kinds of music to assist in their initial efforts. Once it becomes a regular practice many simply seek the silence.

> "We learn to meditate in rhythm with the soul, which is in constant meditation, which is group conscious, which is neither mystical nor limited but is related to the universal Life or energy aspect of the planet as it underlies consciousness and empowers the tendency to love; and which has as its objective, the stimulation of receptive minds and open hearts towards identification with the one Life.

> The objective of occult meditation today is the achievement of a perfect balance between the vertical life of the soul on its Own plane and the horizontal life of the soul-infused personality within the world of men. "Knowing the ways of God and treading the ways of men", the modern disciple, as a mediator meditating the Plan into existence, co-operates with planetary purposes."[14]

If you feel so inclined, find a coach.
Trust and allow that the information in this manual is for you.
Trust that quiet time may allow you to know
What You Really Are.

Once you align with that quiet time and regain full awareness of what you really are, you will have won this Game.

And the planet will be a much better place.

---

[14] "Meditation –a way of life" Lucis Trust website.

Soul—From a Different Perspective

SOUL may be likened to the navigator of one's life. The major challenge is for Kosmic Energy / Consciousness / (You) to stay in tune with Soul's wave. When You have chosen to prepare to embark upon the Game of Life on Earth, certain plans must be made. After all, Earth is a vast playground. For a small but mightily powered energy, plans of choices are to be made. The knowledge and interfacing with the ongoing growth of the entire planetary picture is offered to you (as you plan) and taken into consideration, since everyone desires to be a positive force while in The Game. Merging into the flow in a positive and constructive manner involves careful and concise planning. Upon the finalizing of that core planning, its crux is then given the Life quality of Soul. Each Unit of Consciousness throughout its time on Earth will maintain this blueprint in its possession. As carrier of this blueprint, Soul melds with its Consciousness—YOU. Consciousness and Soul become partners in their intent to enter into, experience, and exit The Game—a winner.

In some regard, Soul may also be likened to what is termed "conscience," the Jiminy Cricket that routinely reminds the Unit of Consciousness, the Kosmic Love Energy, the Beauteous Light (You) as to what was planned prior to entry into this Game. The Game consequently, becomes the protagonist challenging you to remember what it is that's on your blueprint.

In Review

As is witnessed, control has become of paramount importance among nations, groups, and individuals. This condition fosters the loss of Unconditional Love Energy being expressed upon the planet by a majority of its billions of inhabitants. Unconditional Love is an integral and inherent quality of Source.

YOU are not just human. Your physical nature—"man" is illusion. YOU are far more. YOU are Kosmic energy—the provider of the energy enlivening the individual human form. YOU designed and chose each aspect of that vehicle to enable you to function *in accordance with your blueprint*.

How is it that Source and I function?

Jointly! For each is one-and-the-same-(awesome) Energy. One is just far more powerful than the other, with Source being so much more powerful that the only way IT can know of its creation is through ITs stepped-down version—You. Source is best able to know of ITs potential as The Provider and Creator by way of the participants in The Game. Life is so designed that the sensory makeup of your body enables you to intake the multitudinous feelings of the form. Source of All That Is lovingly accepts those very same feelings, simultaneously, instantaneously, and without judgment.

SOURCE takes in the experience as Soul/YOU take on the experience.

The entire Earth phenomenon may be described as a co-creative venture, a venture between the Creator and the Created, in a mode of mutual benefit, both functioning on the levels each is best suited to perform. Each is the enabler of the other—the ultimate and perfect partnership. Again you are FAR more than you think you are.

However, a major problem persists. Upon entry into The Game, the You-side of the partnership loses awareness of the ever-present Partner! This has been a key factor and major problem for nearly all players of The Game. The loss of awareness occurred when you took on the trappings of The Game, i.e., the workshop in relationships. The term "trappings" is far more descriptive than one might first realize, for The Game is in one sense a trap; it quickly mesmerizes each player. (And the term "mesmerize" is also well suited to describe this occurrence.) In one sense, The Game becomes the controller of the participants, who function within a framework of illusion, neither recalling what they really are nor their ability to interact with the field in/on which they are playing.

"The Game is a delight to observe as a member of the audience. In particular, to have the participants grossly and earnestly involved in their efforts, yet not realizing that those efforts have little real bearing on The Game."

The Game is one tough challenge. It has unseen and unsuspected factors interplaying throughout. This is all possible due to the free, creative nature of man. The Game is a kosmic illusion.

The nature of physical man is illusion (but not YOU). The integral system of The Game and the planet involves electromagnetics. The Game is just one of many throughout the Cosmos as we know it.

A theatre-in-the-spherical might just as accurately describe what is taking place, with each player creating their own script moment by moment as she or he walks across the stage.

The Game is not what it seems — it is more. Much more.

Remember also: you're all on the same team!

You have just forgotten.

Actually, it all comes down to the simple but challenging practice of getting quiet.

The glitter and glamour of this workshop is wooing most players away from their original goal: their personal blueprint for this very challenging Game. Most hu-mans are hypnotized and habit-ized by the TV. Video games run a close second, and if not video games, it's the computer and everything it offers. Then, of course, there's the cell phone. The ego is easily addicted to them all. If one intends to win The Game, one must set aside and make use of private, uninterrupted quiet time daily.

To achieve a totally conscious awareness of your connection to the Universe, the key is to go into your quiet place.

Accomplishing this is an extreme personal challenge.

Actually, this is your ultimate challenge **and it is literally an "inside job."**

Achieve this, and you'll win The Game.

Welcome to My Private Place

Here are just some of the many writings that have come to me over the years. I heartily invite and encourage you to develop this skill. It is simple. Merely sit quietly. With writing instrument in hand, permit any thoughts to drop into a special place in the head—that area that the experts say we only use 10-20% of. Late at night or very early morning may be best. You are not recording your regular, ongoing, noisy thoughts relative to the day, someone, or concerns, as is done in journaling.

This involves quietly listening and writing without editing. It's critical to let go of judging the input as you receive it. No one else will ever see it—unless you show it to them. Allow there to be a possibility that you can receive input that you don't consciously put there. Don't expect. Just listen. Some people even invoke input from a guide or whoever is interested in making contact. It might even be God. Placing a question at the top of the paper may be of value. Trust in your ability. It comes in concert with that quiet time we've been referring to. Trust and allow. Accomplishing this skill is simple and not that difficult, really.

They Walk the Stage

They walk the stage.
All across the planet; on sidewalks, dusty roads and rock-strewn vistas.
            Most—asleep.
 Not knowing the truth of their being or the beauty of their nature—except on momentary occasions: the feeling of the warm, soft touch of a child's hand; the sound of carefully created music; the mixture of sunsets and sky. Each potentially touching the soul. Unfortunately—for only a short time. Then... glitter and glamour take precedence.

They walk, run and operate myriad vehicles - chasing myriad goals and purposes—asleep to the truth of what they really are.

Again and again, lost in the fog of confusion brought on by misdirected creativity, they come across the stage—then go into: for them... the unknown.

A strange plot for something as expansive as a planet for a stage and an eternity for the play to run.
(Is this an erroneous conclusion?)
        Conclusion it is not—erroneous, not.
        The plot is ongoing:—conclusion, never.

        Only change and growth.

This **amazing gift** continues to mesmerize me each time I go into it. I find it Kosmically fascinating.

What Is Your Will for Me?

As always, my will is for you to know freedom. To know the freedom of Being. To know Being: free. What it has to offer in open freedom qualities and illusionary freedom aspects.

My will is that you grow unto the full awareness of your potential. The beauty within that potential as it relates to all "others" in all other worlds/kingdoms and the empowering which may take place as result of that awareness as to beauty.

There is a certain quality unsuspected by those in the human condition that is inherent in the beauty of which I speak. It is not possible to be described; only realized, embraced, and used as further strengthening on—to whatever next level you choose to experience.

My will for you is to experience. To have the full library of knowing— thru personal experience those areas of growth possibilities which certain planetary workshops have to offer in the way of experience.

My will is for your understanding to be continuous, toward a more complete knowing which may lead to even further personal awareness which permits further extending and expanding of the part of which you represent to the completion of which I AM.

I would have you know yourself more completely through the discipline of regular meditation that we might more closely commune, as a result of your more consciously being in control of the managerial head of the form in which you reside.

Primarily, my will is for you and all your peers to simply acknowledge my presence within your / their worlds.

My will is that you enjoy your every breathing out and in—of me— thru me—for me. For it is thru you that I am able to enjoy— or—know despair. For, as you perceive your moments and experience them, I also am able to experience.

And now let us rest, or so it would appear. As we find our self in the world of appearances.

Go and enjoy.

Grow — unto Me.

Please

Forever is the period in which you find yourself living.
Finding yourself is the challenge.
Finding yourself in the forever in which you are.
A game: most certainly. Finding oneself is the game.
One's self is the focus in this game. It appears and then
disappears within the daily activities of the game. Its appearance
is dependent upon the extent to which one permits oneself to get
overwhelmed with the glitter and glamour of the "game /
workshop." This game involves illusions of all kinds and sorts.
Most are man-made. Generated from within the manmade mass-
consciousness-formed frameworks that are created by the ongoing
thought patterns of ...man.
Consider the computer, television, radio,
movies, airplanes—
They all take man from his quiet time.
His quiet opening unto himself.
A balance is necessary.
Quiet —— along with the other.
Else it becomes THE GREAT COVER-UP.
These distractions become the end all—be all.
There is nothing more—No time for quiet.
Consequently, man's inner self remains covered up.
The beautiful inner self will not force away the other 'things'; that
is not its nature. It quietly awaits the window of Light that is
provided by quiet time. Committed quiet time.
PLEASE
That is the plea of the inner self.
Quiet please. Somewhere in the day, allow some quiet.

Please.

Doing and Being — a how-to suggestion

Doing is the flip-side of being. Doing on certain levels can be a blending/melding of being. It has been raised to such a level, as in all things: evolution. Doing within a state of being is an ultimate existence for some. Those within the realm of the Master Jesus / Sananda are within that frame of seeking now.

The attempt or journey to do/be is a level of experiencing that is being sought much as your Olympians are seeking a level of perfection/achievement. That is representational of the situation on the higher level of doing/being. Just as your Olympians have displayed extensive practice and routines of developing their individual skills, so must those who seek to achieve the level of going and coming to—wherever, whenever.

To remove one from a trap, one must use great composure, discipline and intent. As an animal who willingly chews off a foot to become extricated from a trap, the call of freedom and being/doing on an extended level calls more strongly than the need for the appendage.

It is the case at this point in the lives of many. A call is being felt (to varying degrees) to extend oneself into a point of discipline that is necessary in order to align the energy points, recognize the truth of what REALLY IS and join with the energy forces which are quietly calling unto those who would hear.

An extending onto the next level to do/be is only a requisite to enable one to move to yet another scale of octaves which offer further challenges.

Awareness knows no bounds.

Enlightenment is an ongoing process. A never-ending process. The ability to Do on a BE level IS. It is similar to those who fly from the great glide path off the white snow into the cold air. They soar. In that moment they know the ability to BE.

To attain that momentary experience they must train, experiment, and do many required activities of the body to enable the soaring to be experienced.

One need only commit to spiritual soaring. Commit to and move toward "being" by quieting the world around and within. When this is done sufficiently and with honest, committed, and surrendered intent—IT IS. The difference: the former is a learned skill, the latter; a recalled state at an expanded degree.

The former is referenced only as a tangible example. The latter is offered as a reminder of what was and is an actuality. Once achieved, it permits one the options to move beyond the confines of the experiential-ized trap of this planetary workshop. It is a very uniquely designed point of experience for spirit. A trap it was not intended to be.

To some—however, it has become.

***That complete came in after I'd been watching the Olympics and had made a remark to Linda as to the probable thrill of the soar in ski jumping.

Tell Me of Me

A spark of beauty. As are all. The fire, while burning brightly within does give off certain beauty that those around may witness when proper abilities are within the viewer. A seeker. A lover of truth. There is so very much to tell ye of ye—for ye are greatly complex in nature as well as in physical makeup.

Those in the medical fields are just now learning the degrees of complexity in which the species called man has been designed and brought into fruition. The desire to be special was also designed into the species. It was a good job and the co-designers who set about to do their very best did just that or so it would seem. Now with the speeding up of the patterning, the species with the greater desire within will be those who will advance on at this now moment. Those without the strong desire to become greater than the mass consciousness would have them be—will only have the other pathway to experience.

It shall all lead to the same point in their/MY formation and destiny for us both. It is such interest to watch the creation on this scale take place and evolve into its final place (for the time being). The Eloi are managing to bring most of the species on to a greater awareness now with the dedicated guide entities along with those who are ever present throughout the total scenario.

What more would you know of this day which moves ever closer to its end in order that a new day may offer yet another opportunity to come over your presence—to grow; to re-unite, to come unto your very own. Forever, the beauty that lies in ALL shows within that which was created to come to know ALL...once again.

A journey of sending out and then——return. The simple story of that which seeks to know more and in the knowing comes to know the vast capability in that knowing. Then the ALL is ever increasing, due to the way in which IT is constructed. The ever-increasing "perpetual motion machine".....now you have it.

There is no end—for IT is an endless, ever on-going phenomenon. The nature of ALL THAT IS, is endless. The ESSENCE of ALL is the TRUTH OF ITSELF. Whatever IT *may seek to be—IT IS. There is no end, for there is no beginning. There will be no end, for there is an ongoing FORCE that shall see that end to be nothing but just another beginning of something even more beautiful; more forceful in its value unto those who seek to know; to understand that FORCE and that ESSENCE which is behind that FORCE.*

§

Water, representing truth, will by its nature move to new levels when allowed.
Truth, within expression, will come to be a carrier of life force, a supporter of further creative expressions, when allowed. Either water or truth, once extended to its ultimate and highest essence, becomes a pearl of wisdom or life-giving droplet unto the receiver. Levels within levels: droplets.......floods. Simply sought: full life experienced. The container of the form: ocean ......experience. The SOURCE of both is the ESSENCE of each. Levels within levels: recognizable on the level each one reaches, yet unlimited – and non-limiting. Powerful and Empowering. Supporting and ever changing. Given an altered stage of circumstantial conditions, i.e., Solid—Elusive, Confinable, uncontrollable; based on volume of accumulation.

This you have yet to fully fathom, for the foremost in factual feasibility flits upon the fast, fleeting fulcrum of faith.

That last line is a sample of the differently constructed and easy to be considered humorous styles of input I received almost routinely. Starting with the same letter of the alphabet - at times, it was too much and I just had to quit, thinking I was making it up. Creativity run amok; methinks.

> This is last for a reason. We need a boost sometimes to
> assist us. It may take the form of: a pulling from up front—
> or a push from the back. Your choice.

The Prism has been altered

*The awakening to the truth of no longer holding old beliefs—as
being advisable, as well as a heart felt directive—is the place of
many untold millions on your planet Earth.*

*The holding to beliefs that by their very evidentiary displays are
lacking in truth lies counter to the Soul and heart of man — now.*

*The obviousness of the chasm between violence and the ways of
love is—everywhere.*
*The frustrations within ones life are the result. "Something is not
right" that little voice says.*
*The sleeper hears it not. Those awakening stir with its message—
and refuse to give support to the beliefs of the past.*
*Technology is not the igniter. It may provide further awakening if
used with great care and selectivity.*
*The days ahead may be likened to the days of Atlantis. The latter
times for Atlantis. Misguided energies impacted that civilization as
well.*
The laws of free will permit it. Mass consciousness permits it.
*This is a place of laws—unseen and unknown (for the most part)
for man has been remiss in seeking them out and putting them to
proper disposal—for his own benefit.*
*We rejoice in bringing this message to hu-man. And we shall be
wondering as to the path(s) he shall take. His options are open and
grand—truly.*
'His' future is as always—his choice.

Bibliography

There are now hundreds of books available for anyone who is sincerely searching. The local library offers many of them. Some of the ones I have read are listed here. I found these to be of great value and collectively they contributed to my own opening. If you are seeking a place to see if what's in this manual could possibly be credible, I suggest *The Holographic Universe*, for starters. If you are technically inclined, Walter Russell unloads a veritable lifetime of study to anyone in his book, *The Secret of Light*. It probably will be a long time before it is outdated. *The Secret Life of Plants* is riveting, along with Masaru Emoto's website. My newsletter offers recommendations as well.

Welcome to the journey and …to **winning**.

* Books by Deepak Chopra (New World)
* Books by Neale Donald Walsh (Hampton Roads & Atria & Putnam)
* Books by Alice Bailey (Lucis Trust)
* Books By Wayne Dyer (Hay House)
* Books by Eckart Tolle (New World Library)

Autobiography of a Yogi by P. Yogananda, (Self-Realization)
As a Man Thinketh by Paul Allen, (Kessinger Publishing)
God I Am by Peter O. Erbe, (Triad Publishers)

From the Heart of a Gentle Brother Bartholemew & Mary Margaret
    Morre (Hay House 1998)
God and the Evolving Universe by Redfield / Murphy, (Putnam)
Hidden Messages in Water by Masaru Emoto, (Atria)
His Light His Love III by Wm Wylie, (Author House)
Initiation by Elisabeth Haich, (Seed Center)
Integral Spirituality by Ken Wilber, (Integral Books/ Shambala)
Journey of Souls by Michael Newton, (Llewellyn Publications)
Joy's Way by Joy Brugh, (Tarcher – Penguin)
Life after Life by Raymond Moody,
Life between Life by Joel Whitton, MD, Ph.D & Joe Fisher (Warner
    Books)
Life of Catherine Of Siena by G. Lamb
Living in the Light by Shakti Gawain, (Whatever Publishing)
Love, Medicine & Miracles by Bernie Siegel, (Harper & Row)
Messages from Michael by Chelsea Q. Yarbro, (Playboy Paper Bk)
Messages from Water by Masaru Emoto, (Atria Book)
Miracles in the Storm by Mark H. Macy, (New American Library)
Power vs Force by David R Hawkins, MD, (Veritas Publishing)
Psyco-Cybernetics by Maxwell Maltz, (Prentice-Hall)
Receiving the Cosmic Christ by Shahan Jon, (Karuna Foundation)
Saved by the Light by Dannion Brinkley, (Harper Collins)
Secrets of the Miracle Inside by Paul McCormick, (Miracle Writers
    LLC)
Space Time and Beyond by Tobin & Wolf, (Bantam NA Books)
The Artists Way by Julia Cameron, (Putnam)
The Celestine Prophecy by James Redfield (Warner Books)
The Divine Matrix by Gregg Braden, (Hay House)
The Everything Meditation Book by R Clark, (Adams Media)
The Emerald Tablets
The Four Agreements by Miguel Ruiz, (Amber-Allen Publ'g)
The Holographic Universe by Michael Talbot (Harper)
The I That Is We by Richard Moss,M.D., (Celestial Arts)
The Keys of Enoch by Dr. J.J. Hurtak,
The Kybalion by Three Initiates (Yogi Publication Society)
The Kyrian Letters by Sandra Radhoff (Heritage Publications)
The Law of Attraction by Esther & Jerry Hicks (Hay House)
The Magic of Believing by Claude Bristol,
The Magic of Findhorn by David Springer & Paul Hawken (Ban-
    tam Books)
The Observing Self by Arthur J Deikman,M.D., (Beacon Press)
The One That Is Both by L.E.Maroski, (iUniverse)

The Prophet by Kahlil Gibran, (A.A. Knopf)
The Quest of the Overself by Dr.Paul Brunton (Weiser)
The Seat ofThe Soul by Gary Zukav(Simon & Shuster)
The Secret Life of Plants by Paul Tompkins and Christopher Bird,
    (Avon)
The Secret of Light by Walter Russell (Univ. Science & Philoso-
    phy)
The Seth Material by Jane Roberts (Bantam Books)
The Nature of Personal Reality by Jane Roberts (Prentice-Hall)
The Silva Mind Control Methods
The Tagore Reader by Chakravarty (Beacon Press)
You Can Heal Your Life by Louise Hay (Hay House)
UFO Contact from the Pleiades by Lt. Col. Stevens, (Genesis)
Vitvan & School of Natural Order

Other publications include:

Sedona—Journal of Emergence published monthly.
What is Enlightenment - published quarterly.
Parabola

Stillness Speaks (a CD) • Eckhart Tolle
The Secret—both a book and DVD

Many others, of course. may be found when one seeks.

Other Resources:

Websites
        www.joyridingtheuniverse.com/   Sheradon Bryce
        www.hado.net   Masaru Emoto
        www.walter-russell.org
        www.sno.org/ Vitvan
        www.lucistrust.org
        www.noetic.org/
        www.circleofa.org   Course in Miracles
        www.ptaah.com   Channeled stuff
        www.firethegrid.org   Shelley Yates' story.
        www.hemisyncforyou.com   Meditation tapes
        www.theinterviewwithgod.com/

If you have any to recommend post them on our blog.

We invite you to gift your friends and other family members with this manual.

Also, inform your favorite non profit as to our open willingness to assist them in their funding efforts.

You may visit our website @ www.onlyuno.com
Our blog is onlyuno.blogspot.com
The folks who have been supportive of this production are both numerous and geographically dispersed.
Our heartfelt appreciation goes out to them all.
Compiling a manual such as this is neither quick nor easy.
Now that you have partaken of this material, it is OUR wish that you tell others about it; all the while move back through it, taking the points which speak to you deep into your being.
As in: meditate.

In the very slight chance this didn't "ring any bells" for you, please pass this Manual on to one of your "weird" friends. They'll come to appreciate and understand their weirdness even better.

And ....We ALL thank you.

We invite you to discover www.onlyuno.com
There we have other options in the reading of more offerings as well as providing you the place to obtain prints of these and other original illustrations by Tim Donahue. We'll be announcing other publications, too.
You may also subscribe to our newsletter AND check out some great links. Contact us, too. We'd like that.
We definitely have fun on our website.

§

You may order additional books from:

Mr. Rrandall Shelton
855 NW Maple Ln.
Redmond, OR 97756-1123

So, in parting:

Set aside the script, for the play writes its own.
That within knows the next scene to be presented
—for there exists no final curtain.

"You know what?

this is NOT the end......

This is the beginning of yet another beginning....

And so IT goes......"

.... "HE" told me so.

Source has assured me of that....often

Light Beings
The Endless Annals. A New Page under the Aura of Mystery and surge of Emotion. An Embryo of Love in the Eternal Moment. Life Spark! The Divine alignment of Spirit/Elements (Energy transformed by Love). A sudden Eternal Alignment: Light; functioning in (for the moment) human form. −TD